D0908875

critters by the Sea

SEA GULLS
IN THE SKY

ELLIOT MONROE

PowerKiDS
press

New York

Published in 2018 by The Rosen Publishing Group, Inc.
29 East 21st Street, New York, NY 10010

First Edition

Editor: Melissa Raé Shofner
Book Design: Tanya Dellaccio

Photo Credits: Cover Sam Ryan Photography/Getty Images; pp. 3–24 (background image) Kemal Mardin/Shutterstock.com; p. 5 Pics4view/Shutterstock.com; p. 7 (top) Claire Louise Gauci/Shutterstock.com; p. 7 (middle) EA Given/Shutterstock.com; p. 7 (bottom) Always Joy/Shutterstock.com; p. 8 Eric Isselee/Shutterstock.com; p. 9 (top) Michael Quinton/Minden Pictures/Getty Images; p. 9 (bottom) RazvanZinica/Shutterstock.com; p. 11 (top) Artsy Imagery/Shutterstock.com; p. 11 (bottom) Stubblefield Photography/Shutterstock.com; p. 13 Peter Kovalev/TASS/Getty Images; p. 14 eilatan/Shutterstock.com; p. 15 fatchul/Shutterstock.com; p. 17 (top) Cory Richards/National Geographic/Getty Images; p. 17 (bottom) Dan Bagur/Shutterstock.com; p. 19 (all) Florian Andronache/Shutterstock.com; p. 21 OFFSTOCK/Shutterstock.com; p. 22 E. O./Shutterstock.com.

Cataloging-in-Publication Data

Names: Monroe, Elliot.
Title: Sea gulls in the sky / Elliot Monroe.
Description: New York : PowerKids Press, 2018. | Series: Critters by the sea | Includes index.
Identifiers: LCCN ISBN 9781538325872 (pbk.) | ISBN 9781538325179 (library bound) | ISBN 9781538325889 (6 pack)
Subjects: LCSH: Gulls–Juvenile literature.
Classification: LCC QL696.C46 M65 2018 | DDC 598.3′38–dc23

Manufactured in the United States of America

CPSIA Compliance Information: Batch #BW18PK: For Further Information contact Rosen Publishing, New York, New York at 1-800-237-9932

CONTENTS

SEA GULLS BY THE SEASHORE

Sea gulls, also called gulls, are a common sight along the shore. If you're at the beach, there's a good chance you'll see some of these birds—especially if the beach is crowded. This is because they love to eat our food!

Gulls have **adapted** to living near people. They've learned that where people gather, food is near. Sometimes they steal food from people. They'll also eat food that people have thrown in the trash.

SEA CREATURE FEATURE

Not all sea gulls live by the sea. Some are found **inland**, far away from the ocean.

Herring gulls are daring! They're known for stealing food right out of people's hands at the beach.

5

BUILT FOR THE AIR AND SEA

There are more than 40 species, or kinds, of sea gulls. From the tip of one wing to the tip of the other, gulls may measure between 24 and 63 inches (61 and 160 cm). This length is called their wingspan.

Sea gulls tend to have mostly white or gray feathers. They also have feet that are perfect for swimming. Folds of skin called webbing connect three long toes in front of each foot and one short toe in back. Their webbed feet act like paddles in the water.

SEA CREATURE FEATURE

Sea gulls are really good at flying. Their wings are the perfect shape for riding air currents. This means they can fly for a long time without **flapping** their wings!

Adult red-billed gulls have bright red feet, legs, and beaks. They're commonly found in New Zealand.

ALL SORTS OF SEA GULLS

There are more than 20 species of sea gulls living in North America. Herring gulls are one of the most common types. These gulls mostly live by the ocean, but many have adapted to living in cities and towns.

Great black-backed gulls are the largest species of sea gull. They can grow to be 31 inches (78.8 cm) long from head to tail. The smallest sea gulls are a species called little gulls. They only grow to be about 11 inches (27.9 cm) long from head to tail.

GREAT BLACK-BACKED GULL

SEA CREATURE FEATURE

Great black-backed gulls live in eastern North America. They're so big, they can swallow small wild ducks whole!

Bonaparte's gulls are the only gulls that build their nests in trees. They're found in North America and spend the summer months in northern Canada and Alaska.

BONAPARTE'S GULL

LITTLE GULL

THEY'LL EAT ANYTHING!

Sea gulls are scavengers. This means they'll eat pretty much anything, including dead animals. They're always searching for food, no matter where they are. Sometimes sea gulls steal food from other gulls. Some even eat sea gull eggs and chicks.

Sea gulls are also opportunistic feeders. This means they'll eat whatever food happens to be closest to them or easiest to get. Gulls that live by the ocean eat fish, snails, clams, and other shellfish. Sea gulls break open shellfish by dropping them from high up.

SEA CREATURE FEATURE

Swallow-tailed gulls live around the Galápagos Islands and other islands off the coast of South America. They're the only type of gull that sleeps during the day and hunts for food at night.

Gulls that live inland will often gather in places where people throw away food. **Landfills** are one of their favorite places to visit.

SWALLOW-TAILED GULL

OUT AT SEA

People sometimes see sea gulls following fishing boats. Large groups of gulls may fly around a single boat, waiting for people to toss food or fish over the side. When fishermen aren't looking, gulls may even fly down and take fish from their nets.

Many animals can't drink salt water, but sea gulls can. They have special body parts above their eyes that remove the salt from their bodies. Gulls also drink freshwater found in rivers and lakes.

SEA CREATURE FEATURE

Some kinds of sea gulls will dive into the water to catch fish. Others will steal fish from pelicans.

People working on fishing boats may view sea gulls as pests. Gulls may steal fish right off the boat deck!

TALKING AND TRAVELING

Sea gulls **communicate** using movements and sounds. A long trumpetlike call means a herring gull is going to refuse to move. Herring gulls will also try to make themselves look bigger when they're angry.

Most sea gulls live in the same place all year. However, some gulls from colder parts of the world **migrate**. Laughing gulls, for example, spend the summer in the northeastern United States. When the weather turns colder, they fly south to spend the winter in Florida, South America, or Central America.

SEA CREATURE FEATURE

During migration, some gulls may wander off and end up far away from their normal nesting grounds. This may lead to different species of gulls **mating**.

Sometimes sea gulls migrate in large groups. Tens of thousands of gulls may fly together.

BUILDING A NEST

Once a year, in the spring, most sea gulls come together to mate. Mated sea gulls will stay together for years. In the winter, however, mated gulls sometimes join different groups. They often return to the same nest site each year and will find each other again in the spring.

Most sea gulls build their nests in the ground or on cliff sides. Nests are built so predators and people have a hard time reaching them. They may be made of sticks, seaweed, and other plants.

SEA CREATURE FEATURE

Sea gulls such as black-headed gulls and herring gulls have adapted to live in cities. Gulls that live in cities often build their nests on rooftops.

Some species of sea gulls will create nesting colonies such as the one shown here. Nesting colonies are places where large groups of gulls build their nests close together. Sometimes gulls nest with other types of birds, too.

SEA GULL CHICKS

After building a nest, a female sea gull will lay two to four eggs. Mated sea gulls take turns sitting on the eggs to keep them warm. After 20 to 30 days, the sea gull chicks will **hatch** out of their shells.

Chicks remain in their parents' nest for about six months. Their parents take good care of them. When it's time to eat, parent gulls chew and swallow food, then bring it back up to give to the chicks.

SEA CREATURE FEATURE

Young gulls are often born with brown or gray feathers. They'll **molt** each year until they grow their adult feathers. This can take up to four years for larger species.

Baby sea gulls are called chicks. Young gulls are called juveniles. Feather coloring is different for chicks, juveniles, and adults, as these yellow-legged gulls show.

CHICK

JUVENILE

ADULT

19

GULLS HELPING PEOPLE

Since 1995, the California gull has been the official state bird of Utah. California gulls are found along the Pacific coast as well as farther inland. Stories tell of California gulls that saved Utah's **Mormon** settlers by eating grasshoppers that were destroying their crops in 1848.

The relationship between sea gulls and people is not simple, though. More and more sea gulls have started living in cities and towns. Sea gull droppings and nests may ruin rooftops. Gulls can also be a danger to low-flying airplanes.

SEA CREATURE FEATURE

Sea gulls keep our beaches clean by eating dead fish along the shore.

Fishermen may find good fishing spots by following gulls out to sea.

PROTECTING SEA GULLS

In the past, some sea gull species were in danger of going **extinct**. Gull feathers were once used to make hats. Today, few people would consider eating a sea gull. At one time, however, people ate sea gull eggs and chicks.

People have passed special laws to protect sea gulls. The New Jersey Conservation of Wildlife Law, passed in 2000, has helped gull populations grow. Still, sea gulls survive mainly because they're great at adapting to live alongside people.

GLOSSARY

adapt: To change to suit conditions.

communicate: To share ideas and feelings through sounds and motions.

extinct: No longer existing.

flap: To move up and down or back and forth.

hatch: To break open or come out of.

inland: Land that is away from the coast or border.

landfill: A place where garbage is buried.

mate: To come together to make babies.

migrate: To move from one place to another as the seasons change.

molt: To shed hair, feathers, shell, horns, or skin.

Mormons: Members of a church that was founded in the United States by Joseph Smith in 1830.

INDEX

WEBSITES

Due to the changing nature of Internet links, PowerKids Press has
developed an online list of websites related to the subject of this book.
This site is updated regularly. Please use this link to access the list:
www.powerkidslinks.com/seac/gull